SEE DAVE WORK.

BY PATRICK KENNEDY

SEE.

SEE DAVE.

SEE DAVE WORK.

Wake up, wake up!
Dave wake up!
It's time.
Time to go to work.
Dave, go to work!

Don't eat breakfast. No, no.
No time Dave, no.
No breakfast today!

See, Dave, see!
Traffic is fun!
Everyone is here.
Everyone is excited to go to work!

You are late Dave.
Late, late, late!
You should have woken up earlier.
Dave, you should have been up early!
Sneak, Dave, sneak!

Phone is ringing Dave!
Don't answer, finish your email.
Dave, submit your paperwork!
Everyone is watching.
Everything is important, Dave!

Rumble rumble.
Dave you are hungry!
No time to eat, Dave.
Work, work, work.
No time for lunch!

No time to clean your Inbox.
No, no.
No time at all.
So much to do.
Do it!
Do it Dave! All of it!

Stop being so sleepy Dave!
Catch up on your calls.
Appearance is important, Dave.
Sit up straight Dave, sit up Dave!

Have some dinner.
Eat, eat!
Cram the food in!
No time to waste. No time, no time!

About the Author

Well, that about sums it up.

www.ingramcontent.com/pod-product-compliance
Lightning Source LLC
Chambersburg PA
CBHW041535280526
45792CB00004B/1518